THINK OF ME

Nicholas Trandahl

Winter Goose
PUBLISHING
where words take flight
wintergoosepublishing.com

Winter Goose Publishing
45 Lafayette Road #114
North Hampton, NH 03862

www.wintergoosepublishing.com
Contact Information: info@wintergoosepublishing.com

Think of Me

COPYRIGHT © 2018 by Nicholas Trandahl

First Edition, February 2018

Cover Design & Formatting by Winter Goose Publishing

ISBN: 978-1-941058-77-0

Published in the United States of America

To Britt, Lily, Holly, and Story

CONTENTS

STILL SO WILD

I love all of this—
all of you.
And yet there's a part of me
that's still so wild.

I could walk deep
into the forest gloom
and never come back.

QUEEN CITY

Once, when I was younger,
I meditated on top of a mountain,
and I buried sandalwood prayer beads
with my bare hands.

Sunlight was streaming down—
a luminous cascade.

The earth kissed the sky.

It was so still and quiet
that I could almost hear
the roots of the pine trees
burrowing deeper—
weaving amongst prehistory.
Beyond the roots,
in the dark womb of the earth,
granite stones were grinding together—
excited for their own chance to bloom
from the rust-colored pine needles
in some distant age to come.

In the pines on the mountainside,
I imagined the solemn faces
of the fallen Crow warriors
that were slain there by the Sioux.
That peak is a tomb—
a holy place.

Once, on my way to the top,
a doe and I surprised one another.
We probably never crossed paths again.
Our lives are in different places now,
but we still love the same mountain.

Somewhere far down below
there was a garden where, as a child,
I picked raspberries and rhubarb—
my teeth crunching the tart stalks.
There were always snakes to find
within the flowerbeds.

Everything's different now.
This summer the mountain burned.
The roots have grown still—
blackened.

The snakes are harder to find.

The garden is overgrown.

DEITY OF NIGHT

There's that moment—
the last of the day's light
draining out beyond
the western brim of the world.

The moon, I can tell,
is shining fiercely
behind the unkempt clouds—
illuminating with argent fire
their wispy edges.

It's the blazing eye
of the deity of night.

The sky is a mask she wears
to whisper poems to me
in the cool summer dark.

Listen . . .

TURBULENCE

The descent into Boston.
A thick soupy fog—
some New England murk.

Slight turbulence.

A glowing sliver of dawn
so artfully sliced
into the Atlantic horizon.

A SQUIRREL IN OAK BLUFFS

The cobalt blue of the Atlantic
just through those trees—
glistening points of brightness.

Gulls crying out in the air.

Sunlight is splattered
upon the grass and quiet lanes—
upon the fallen leaves.

We're not from here,
but I'm watching my wife
crouching down
at the edge of a yard
in peaceful Oak Bluffs—
rusty orange leaves drifting down.
She coaxes a grey squirrel
from an old oak—
its branches splayed
against the October sky.

I take a photograph
of the squirrel and her.

I smile—
I'm sure I smile.

How could I not?

BLESSED TO THE ANKLES

We walked along the shore
towards nowhere.
I'm unsure who led the way—
maybe we walked side by side.
I carried her shoes.
We strode across the empty shells
and the desiccated crabs.
We admired things we found—
treated everything like a treasure.
I removed my leather oxfords
and my socks—
a white lace of Atlantic foam
sighed across the shore
with each gentle wave.
Our bare feet
were blessed to the ankles
by things we couldn't ever
take home with us.

TOMBSTONES AT EDGARTOWN

Edgartown is an old whaling town
on Martha's Vineyard's eastern shore—
big white houses tucked against the sea.
When we first went to Edgartown,
clouds rolled in over a brassy sunset.
We hiked over the sand and beach grass
in the windy dusk, to the lighthouse.
When we next went to Edgartown,
we visited the old cemetery there.
Many of the tombstones
were corroded by brine—
centuries of salty sea air.
Moss and lichens covered some
like the granite boulders back home.
There were four old graves
lined up in a row—
a family.
The husband and wife
died in their later years,
but their two sons were both lost at sea
a year apart from one another—
in consecutive Octobers.
Can you imagine the sorrow and silence
of that New England island home
in the years after those boys died?
I imagine the rooms dark and cold—
grey Atlantic light seeping in
through unwashed windows—
no more laughter of strong young men

eager to try their hand at whaling
in the cobalt vault of the sea—
just two silent parents
mourning their broken lives
as age overtakes them far too quickly.

BEER BOTTLE MOAN

Camping—
late October.

Turkeys on the far bank—
trout in the creek.

Sitting beside the tent—
bare feet in dead oak leaves.
An empty beer bottle—
the beer was dark and rich
and tasted of maple.
The autumn wind moans
as it enters the bottle.

A sunny afternoon—
almost warm but not quite.
Feathery clouds—
a cool blue sky.
Oak leaves drifting—
a chilled wind.

Another beer bottle moan.

The turkeys have gone away.

THE FIRST FLAKES

This is it.
A hush in the birds
that haven't gone south—
low-hanging clouds
sliding in from the northwest
on grey icy winds—
a heavy sky.

The first flakes.

SOUP IN THE DESERT

Winter chill.

Cold desert morning—
somewhere outside El Paso.

Gloves on—
camouflage layers.

Hungry cold soldiers
gathered around the mess tent
like weathered hobos
on Skid Row.

Each one of us are given
a ladleful of hot soup
in a Styrofoam cup.

No utensils—
drinking the soup
with one gloved hand,
and cradling an M-16
in the other.

The second-best meal
I've ever had.

STATE LINE

The frayed edge
between two flyover states
that I've haunted for years.

Every highway exit
has some significance—
some shard of memory.

The sun is falling
behind the mountain—
blue winter shadows.

I feel something here.

WHAT A NEW DAY
HAS TO OFFER

The snow comes and goes
in flourishes of cold wind
until, at dusk, it grows tired
of all the coming and going,
and it decides to stay.

The day has a chilled soul.
Hundreds of coal miners
were sent home without jobs
in the morning's cold ache—
one of them is my brother.

The dusk grows blue—
everything looks submerged.
The snow will continue
into the expanse of tomorrow,
and I wonder what a new day
has to offer to any of us.

CUSP

A kind spring breeze moves
in the shadows of the bedroom.
It's the middle of the morning,
and I'm holding my wife in bed.
The window curtains flow
like they're underwater.
The click of the ceiling fan
is the only sound at first,
but then the edge of a curtain
licks the strings of my acoustic guitar
that stands in the corner of the room—
one of its strings is broken,
and the instrument is neglected.

I bought that acoustic guitar
when I was completely broken,
but looking for my next steps.
It was early December,
but the Middle Eastern summer
and military inpatient wards in autumn
were fresh on my skin and my mind.
My first marriage was aflame,
and I had a room in a basement
in a South Dakota college town.
I remember when I first felt
the cool black body of that guitar—
absently strummed those strings
that weren't yet broken or dirty.
I hoped it could mean something

or somehow ignite a change in me—
an ember in the tinder of my ribs.
I was wearing a thin black jacket
that I bought down in El Paso
and a green and brown scarf
around my slender stalk of a neck.
The guy running the guitar shop
said that I reminded him of a beatnik—
all cool and poor in postwar New York
with a joint in thin lips, an empty wallet,
and poetic desire itching out.
But I wasn't a beatnik or a pothead,
and I bought the guitar with cash.

I walked out of the basement shop,
a brand-new guitar case
pleasantly full upon my back,
and I climbed a stairwell
up onto the sidewalk on Main Street.
The sky was an imperfect white—
heavy with the promise of winter.
A bit of snow was whispering down.
I had a yellow journal in my pocket
that my sister sent to me
when I was deployed—
yellow has always calmed me.
That journal was steadily filling up
with my amateurish attempts at poetry.
Those first poems wouldn't be published
until four years later.

What an amazing time that was

to still be drawing breath-—
so vulnerable and full of possibility.
I was in my prologue back then—
I was on the cusp of becoming
something better.

THINGS WE CAN NEVER OWN

Between Upton and Sundance,
a bluebird flies in front of my car
almost every single time
I reach the county line.
There's so much wildlife there—
magpies and crows;
people are always hitting deer.
I'm arrogant enough to think
that it's the same bluebird each time—
trying to tell me something.
But that's the way of us, isn't it?
We hear the fabled voice of God
or the tongues of the universe
bending our collective ears
and whispering messages to us
in just about anything.
That's the way of humanity—
to make a bit of meaning out of nature.
That's why we immortalize the sun
that sets every single day of the year,
and the imperfection of an apple,
and the plumpness of a nude hip,
and the voices that aspen leaves use
when a summer wind rustles them.
That's why we create art and poetry
about things that act apart from us.
The only thing we're capable of doing
is fabricating purpose and voice
to all the things we can never own.

WARLORD

I'm ten or eleven years old,
waiting in the grasslands
under a cloudless blue sky.
We stand beside
a row of parked cars—
it's unsafe to stray away.

Low distant rumble—
a dark herd of bison
flows over a ridge—
a tobacco-colored flood.
Herded by cowboys,
the colossal herd
passes just before us.
A fog of dust and snorts—
summer's deep shudder.

A lone bull, a straggler,
stands there for a moment
in the tan cloud of dust.
He looks at us—
the tragic warlord of the plains.

How did all this happen?
he seems to inquire.

And then the bison turns
to follow the sea of history—
a brown silhouette fading

into more shades of brown.

The air is fossilized.

SOMETHING I CAN'T
PRETEND TO UNDERSTAND

I was in the Bighorn Mountains,
on the thickly-forested slopes
above Meadowlark Lake.
There were fallen trees
that were so damp and rotted
that they crumbled underfoot.
My firstborn daughter
was strapped upon my back,
her tiny fat legs dangling.
It was her first summer.
She had been born in December—
on Christmas Eve.
We ascended into a realm
of towering pines and large moose.

If I should die today or tomorrow
or half a century from now,
I'll be able to contentedly say
that at that breathless moment
I was there—

I was truly there.

My spirit was practicing its ascent
into something I can't pretend to understand.

THE STONES OF VIRGINIA WOOLF

It's nearly April,
and the grass is greener—
buds are evident in the trees.
Today it's been pouring rain,
and the sky has been thick
with a soupy grey sheet of cloud.

On this day back in 1941,
Virginia Woolf walked into a river
with some heavy stones
filling the pockets of her clothes.
She didn't come back out of the river
until her life had gone away—
swept downstream to the sea
between England and France.
I always admired her
for the end that she chose.
I'd probably catch some criticism
for saying that she was brave,
but I will anyway—
Virginia Woolf was brave.
It would've been the hardest thing
for her to not spill the stones
from her sodden pockets
and swim up to the flowing surface—
breathless and cold, but alive.
But she never would've found
whatever it was she was looking for—

I hope she found it there at the end.
I hope she found it in the waves—
her stones her anchors
holding her fast to an ending
and some mysterious beginning.

PERFECTLY HONEST

This evening, as the spring rain fell,
I found a new favorite poem—
"Zona" by Jim Harrison.
I found it in his final collection.
Words can be perfectly honest,
just like the sudden glare of lightning
or the rushing tide of wind
that pushes down the prairie grass.
Spring nights should be like that.
My friend Frank, in New York,
said it's a night to put red wine
into a cheap plastic cup.
It must not be storming
all the way over there.

NATURE WORDS

The world is broken.
But if it wasn't
I'd say that I'd be grinning
when you came upon me
out in the warm summer woods—
shafts of emerald light
pouring down on me,
a full pack upon my back
and walking stick in my grip.
I'd whisper secrets to you—
things about the world,
things I'd discovered
that maybe you hadn't yet.
And you might smell pipe smoke
upon all the nature words
that drift from the nest
of my russet beard
like pine pollen in the summer air.
I'd raise a fistful of moss
to my eager nose,
and then I'd raise it to yours.
In a world that wasn't broken
we'd fill our lungs with gods.

BREAKFAST AT CAMP

The tea kettle
sits in the hot ashes—
little orange embers still smoldering.
The kettle begins to hiss—
soon it'll be ready
for mugs of hot tea.

Gentle quiet morning—
weather still cool.

I started a campfire at sunrise.
Now I put a cast-iron skillet
on the leftover coals.
Always avoid direct flames
when cooking breakfast at camp—
an outdoors tip from Hemingway.

Thick-cut maple bacon
coated in coarse black pepper—
I cut in half a whole package of it
and layer it in the skillet.

Ah, that precious sizzle—
those little bubbles
rising in the runny grease.

A fine breakfast.

BEFORE HER

for Brittany

I feel like, before her,
I was never really alive.

I certainly wasn't a poet.

MAY DAY

Sunday church bells
echo across Canyon Lake.
I bet if the sun could speak,
it would sound like the bells.

A goose with her goslings
out on the surface of the lake—
we watch them from the shore.

My kids harvest cherry blossoms—
I linger,
plucking my own blooms
when they move on.

A man should be as curious
about the world's gifts
as his children are.

ETERNALLY ASCENDING

dedicated to the passengers and crew
of EgyptAir Flight 804

Maybe all of you disappeared
into the early morning moonlight—
sixty-six tired hearts released
to fly up into the Egyptian dawn
as if you were migrating swallows—
eternally ascending.

I wonder if your clothes
still smelled of Paris—
your breath still flavored
with coffee and kisses?

If I could fly seven miles up,
I would want to collect a story
from each one you,
give each one of you a hug
and tell you that everything's okay
but also that nothing at all
will ever be the same again.

FULL

My wife cooked dinner for us
at our old kitchen stove—
just she and I.
Chicken cordon bleu
with green beans sautéed in bacon—
we drank cold Sauvignon blanc.

Afterwards, outside in the dark,
we smoked cigars and drank wine
in the caress of the cool night.
In the shadows of our driveway,
we fucked on the hood of the car—
watchful for passing cars.

There were stars and smiles—
the night was a full one.

AN EFFORT TO FEEL

When I was a new soldier
going through basic training,
I watched a man smile wildly
as he shattered his foot
against a concrete wall—
kick after kick.

When I was leaving the Army
after my deployment,
my Middle Eastern tragedy,
soldiers were still trying
to destroy themselves
in an effort to feel something.

By that time,
I was one of them.

SPEAK TO ME

I went outside—
under the trees
and the storm.

I just needed
to hear something
speak to me.

EASTERN VOICES

dedicated to Jim Harrison

Intermittent rains—
a June thunderstorm.
Petrichor arrives in a sudden rush,
like the first sip of a cocktail—
a cool reprieve from the heat.
The thirsty earth is swallowing
a thickening sky.
The East speaks with wet wide lungs,
and we worship the voices of all the gods
in one deep breath.

BIRCH TREES

Today I read how, at night,
the white limbs of birch trees
have been found to droop down
as if the trees were slumbering,
and then they arise again at dawn.
There's something so pleasing
about that sylvan revelation.
It's good to know that the birches
aren't that dissimilar from me—

that we both thrive in the sun
and also in the summer rain—

that we both know when it's time
to settle in for the evening
and when it's time to awaken.

ON THE HORIZON

The deer and rabbits
are slamming themselves
beneath the tires
of the cars and trucks.
Look up ahead—
there's one hell of a storm
on the horizon, and we're all
headed towards it.

DANDELIONS AND WATERMELON

for my daughters

The start of summer
means you're going away.

And so we're holding
ruby red slices of watermelon.
She holds a bouquet of dandelions—
yellow like lemon peels.
We're happy,
or we're trying to be—
trying to act that happy
to keep from weeping.

Please, my daughters,
I need you to remember this.
Hold this with you,
like I will.

We can do one last thing
before you go away—
let's make a ton of wishes
and watch them all come true
in a couple months or so.

FALL APART TOGETHER

I'll make us a drink—
we'll fall apart together.

We'll run away to a city
where we can get lost.

We can make believe
that everything's okay.

SPARKS

We're simply hollowed out people
as we drive across the state line—
down into Colorado.
I'm smoking a small cigar
and reading some Ginsberg.
The rugged spine of the Rockies
fills up the passenger window.
It's summer, but the snow still gleams
up on the peaks and in the saddles.
The mountains are distant but watchful—
like slumbering titans.
My wife says they look fake
with their perfect white crowns—
she says they look painted
onto the blue canvas of the sky.
Maybe we'll see some things
that will change us—
maybe those mountains,
maybe the gleaming heart
of downtown Denver,
maybe time with dear friends.
Maybe something meaningful
will strike some sparks
from the cold flint
of our broken hearts.

PLACE TO PLACE

City lights glitter like magic.

The great sweep of the city
never ever stops—
not even for a minute.

She loves it.

She says that in the city,
even at midnight,
it's impossible to feel alone.
The hordes are always awake—
always traveling from place to place.

RUINS

for Samantha Sullivant

With just a few earnest words
years of bitterness drifted away—
weary and barely visible,
forgetful of how it had been birthed
mewling into the world.
I'd like to think
that all that bitterness changed
when it ascended out into space—
when it set down the weight
of the whole damn world.
Let's gather it up
and build something new
out of the ruins.

NIGHTTIME IN QATAR

Nighttime in Qatar—
nerves were shot long ago.

Three fingers of rum
in a plastic cup—
I drop in a couple Vicodin
and take a pull.

When I walk later,
trying to get to my bed,
the desert and the night
slide away from me—
a hot blurry world.

My life is tilting—
precariously.

There are no gods here—
only punishment
and solitude.

A death is written up there—
in the vastness of the stars
that I can't see anymore.

TEN DAISIES

It's a quiet summer—
a solemn one.
It's a season of stillness,
and I've got to hunt
for anything to appreciate—
I frequently return home
empty-handed.
So, I've pinned ten daises
to the edge of my heart.
I love them from a distance—
bunched together like siblings
next to our front sidewalk.
They shiver in the summer rain,
and they shiver in the sunshine
because a breeze moves them.
From their place at the edge of the yard,
they nod their ten petaled heads
at all the cars and trucks—
all the passersby.
They're rooted but always moving.
They might be more alive
than I can manage to be.
They've a lot to teach me,
those ten daises,
about how to bloom
and how to be resilient.
Those ten daises are there,
day after day
and night after night,

dancing so subtly
in the heat and the light.

A GIFT OFFERED

I adore that woman,
and not only because
of how she looks
in her new swimsuit
or because she drinks
brandy and ice
out of a damn jar
on a hot summer day—
my beautiful girl.

I adore her because
she has given me
her whole heart
and has taken mine
like a gift offered.

EVERYTHING NATURAL

The clouds are broken up
in the last of the fading light.
The pines surrounding the campsite
are tall and venerable,
and I'm sure that they've heard
all sorts of sylvan secrets
throughout the centuries.
There are also scattered oaks—
a luminous shade of green
and younger than the pines.
Orange light from the campfire
flickers across their features.
It starts to rain again—
the fire sizzles hotly.
Good things are gathered here
in the beginning of the night—
the day's last murmur.

In the warmth of morning
I'm gently awoken by the golden sun
painting the east wall of the tent.
Next to me, my wife still slumbers.
Good morning, sweetheart, I whisper to her—
almost too quiet to hear.
Good morning in the forest.
Her eyes are still shut,
their coffee-brown depths hidden.
But still she smiles, and that is enough—
it's always enough.

Later in the afternoon,
the rain drums ceaselessly
upon the outside of the tent.
We make love quietly and intensely,
and then she falls asleep.
I'm reading some poetry,
but then I take a break
to listen to the rainstorm.
This is peace—
imprisonment in a tent
with a book of good poems
and my one true love
in the throes of postcoital slumber.
I pray to the clouds
which are spilling their evidence
in cool hearty abundance.
I pray that the afternoon rain
isn't yet slowing down,
but I'm afraid that it is.

Later, after the rain,
the forest is quickly drying.
The ants have gone to hide
in their dry tunnels,
but now the flies are out.
Life comes and goes
like an ocean tide.
The sun is falling—
its warm touch presses
through the oak leaves
and paints the side of my face.
The leaves are glowing

with emerald light—
like green stained glass
at a Sunday Catholic Mass.
These woods are church then, I suppose—
the fervent cast of divinity.
And everything natural is blessed
and is also a blessing.

A LITTLE HISTORY

My mind is a soft sky—
pale yellow and pink.

But pastel lilac blossoms
are falling on skulls
long collecting moss.

There is ruin here.

TRYING TO GET TO ABU NAKHLAH

Relaxing on a bunk
in an air-conditioned tent
on a base in Kuwait.
It was summer—
hotter than hell.
I was in transit—
trying to return to my duty station
in some other hellhole country
in the Middle East.
I'd been alone for over a week—
trying to hitch a ride
on a southbound cargo plane
to get to Abu Nakhlah.

Still no flight out—
nothing to do
but read a book
of Old Icelandic sagas
that I'd brought with me
from back home.
Just reading those sagas—
day after day.
Waiting.

Meanwhile . . .

Bragi looked down from Asgard—
Who amongst the Persians

is reading the old legends?

His wife, Idunna, kissed him—
her sweet breath tasting of apples.
Turn away from coarse Midgard, husband,
and make love to me.

I was still waiting.

Odin was wandering the desert—
a raven on each shoulder,
and one eye a bottomless pit.

Maybe I'd never leave that place.

THISTLE AND QUARTZ

Alone—
climbing wooded hills
for the sake of nothing
but the climb itself.
Or perhaps there's something to find
up there in the wild loft
of the pinewoods.

Sounds fade away—
humanity's singular bellow
diminished to a muted whisper
and then to nothing.
Tranquility grows here
among the tall pines—
so does a single perfect thistle,
purple like an amethyst
among the rusty pine needles.

Deeper I climb.
The pines are older here—
larger.
Ascending a granite ridge.
Nearby, a startled whitetail buck
bounds through the deadfall.

There are pieces of rose quartz—
pale pink in the daylight.
They're scattered
on a bed of green moss.

I find a perfect shard of crystal
to take back home with me,
and I rub away the dirt with spit—
admire its ripened pink—
the color of a rare steak.

The summit of exposed granite—
lichen-covered
and pale like a skull.
I look out over the valley—
sky colored like slate.
There are no geese in the air—
it's too early in the year.
Now there's nothing left
but the descent back to camp.

I pass that same thistle
on my way back down,
and nod at it in recognition.

ETCHING (MISSED CHANCES)

Last night I dreamt
that I was in New York City,
walking with some people—
faces I can't make out.

It was night.

I found a quote by Bukowski
that was crudely etched
into a metal scaffold in an alley.
Maybe he carved it himself
with a dull pocketknife—
cigarette hanging from his lips
and whiskey on his breath.

I can't remember what it said,
but I'm pretty sure
that it possessed the power
to change my life—
to snap me out of something
or warn me of something.
However, I did discover on thing:

we can miss chances—
even in our sleep.

ABIDE

It's six in the evening
but still as bright as noon—
around eighty-five degrees.
There are kids in swimsuits
flying past my house
on their shiny new bikes—
obviously heading for the pool.
I'm sitting here after work,
still wearing my tie and shirtsleeves,
in the late shade beside my home—
sipping a citrusy gin and tonic
until my lips are a little numb
and my cheeks are aching
from wanting to grin.

I am happy.

Freshly-read poems are rattling around
in the vault of my skull,
hooking themselves against my synapses—
each flavor becoming ingrained
in the work that I'll pound forth
on the keys of my old typewriter
when I head back inside.

The contents of my tumbler
have dwindled to perilous lows,
and just a thin layer of fluid remains
with a few bright slices of lemon and lime.

I'm not like those kids on their bikes
that are going to the swimming pool.

I'm not going anywhere—
I'm no seeker.

No, I'm just sitting out here,
and the breeze is cool.

I'm fine here.

GIVING A LIAR MONEY

I'd taken my wife out to dinner—
both of us had steaks,
and I had some bourbon to drink.
Outside the restaurant,
a young homeless man
tried to sell me gravel
that was wrapped in metal wire.
He said he needed some cash
to take a girl he liked out for a meal.
No thanks, I told the boy.
My wife felt terrible for him.

After we'd driven away
I was angry at that young man—
angry with him for lying to me.
There was no dinner date—
there was no girl.
Why couldn't he have told us
the truth of his needs?
I would've given him cash
if he'd just said he was hungry
or that he was trying to get somewhere.
I knew that I was being lied to—
I can tell when I'm being bullshitted.

This encounter was some time ago now,
but I'm still haunted by that boy.
I think of him dead somewhere—
a hot place and far from home.

I think of him in prison
because he stole food or money.
I guess these days I wonder
if it's wrong to give a liar money—
especially if he's desperate.

Every single day priests and politicians lie.
Poets lie—
poets are paid for books
that are saturated in lies and fantasies.
The boy had rocks and wire.
I have ink and paper
and a company to publish it.
Our shadows on the asphalt
of that restaurant's parking lot
were identical in the hot sun.

BUT STILL

The bottom is falling out
of the whole fucking world,
and every one of us knows it.

But still—

the twilight leans into me
like a childhood friend—
all lavender and orange
and blushing with stars.
And the moon is playful—
the way it dashes
behind the dark clouds
and back out again.

A NIGHT IN DEADWOOD

The sound of the shuffle—
the feel of it in my hands.
The casinos are down the hill,
but we're dealing cards
with a graceful slide
across a dining room table.
Beer, wine, and cocktails
keep coming from the kitchen.
Between hands we smoke cigars
out in the backyard,
under a mist of stars.
I piss in an alley—
smiling drunkenly.
I want to howl at the moon.
The ember of my cigar glows—
placing little orange hints
upon my face and beard.
The scent of pine drifts down
from further up the hill
in the summer night.
It comes from the cemetery—
the legendary dead,
folk heroes all.
There are offerings on the graves
of liquor and playing cards—
a single bullet.

MY BONES ARE COMING HOME

Driving up into the Bearlodge
snaking our way up
into lofty woodlands.
The aroma of the ponderosas
fills the summer-flavored wind
that breaks over our rushing car.

The pines are starting to give ground
to thickets of bright leafy aspens—
a lake is up ahead.

My bones are coming home.

I think the stars and the trees
conspired to forge me
in the luminous qualities
at the beginning.
My form was different then—

brighter.

CLIFF SWALLOW TRAIL

dedicated to Robert Frost

Late summer.

Hiking through tall ferns—
gently-whispering aspens.
Occasionally there's an old pine—
a wise steward of the forest
in a cloak of mint green moss.

Rambunctious roots yield
to the hush of the tall pines—
a wild cathedral.
There's a piousness to pine—
such solemnity and stillness.
A few whistled notes echo back
through the forest depths.

The trail narrows.
One path becomes many—
faint and branching.
There's a growing doubt,
and a nagging fear of being lost.
Hiking down the one less-traveled—
an overgrown ribbon
that crosses a small stream.
The walking stick stabs deep
into the dark cool mud.

A whitetail fawn silently steps

from a sunlit meadow.
It follows for a while—
a curious sylvan ghost.
Up ahead, there's a trail marker—
it was indeed the right path.

Following a creek upstream
to the north side of the lake—
blue-green and glittering
in the noonday sun.
A canoe and a kayak
drift about on the lake's surface
like lazy water bugs.
The trail comes to an end.

A jaunt back to the campsite.
Settling down for lunch—
a salami and cheese sandwich
and a cold bottle of amber ale
to wash down the dryness.

Cigar smoke in the forest air.

THE MUSIC OF WYOMING

Sitting outside
in the early September dark.
I know it's almost fall
because of all the seasonal beer
that fills a shelf in the fridge—
all the orange and brown labels.
All the best flavors—
maple, nutmeg, cinnamon, pumpkin.
I could hear a train earlier—
the music of Wyoming.
But it's long gone now,
heading towards Moorcroft
and the coal mines beyond.
The only sound left
when the train has faded
is the electric strain
of the nearby streetlight.

THIS ISN'T A POEM

Things are just quietly existing
like the stars in the night sky
and the leaves in the trees—
always aloof of plots.

There's my typewriter—
quiet and heavy on my desk.

There's a tumbler—
empty but for the lemon slices
that rest in the bottom
in a shallow slick of fluid.

There's the smell of trout
sautéed in my favorite pan—
lemon pepper and sea salt to season.

There's the taste of a cigar
still acrid on my tongue.

There's the rumpled sheets
in our darkened bedroom
that smell of recent sex—
the air faintly humid
from our exertions.

There's the soft curve of her hip—
her bare back to me
and her heavy breathing

rhythmic with slumber.

There's a wind gusting outside
in the cloudless night
and stars shining beyond the leaves—
especially that red star
that's been smoldering like an ember
on the southern horizon
for the last couple weeks.

There's the tall old cottonwoods
hissing their chaotic dirge
at the death of summer,
and I am quite sure
there are few sounds
better than the leaves.

There's the quietude
of this household
in the heart of the night.

There's the last thought
before the descent into the dreams
that I won't remember
when the morning comes.

OF MOSS AND SOIL

In another life I could be snapped
from the limbs of society.
I'd fall to the forest floor
and seep into the loam.
Only burrowing animals
could ever find me,
and also the slow roots
reaching out endlessly.
I'd never be consumed by wildfires,
and my solitude would taste
of moss and soil.

THE FIRST DAY OF AUTUMN

I'm reading Longfellow poems
from a small tattered book—
at least a century old.
The fragile pages are yellowed,
and the cover is bound in cloth.
The book feels as delicate as a bird.

A chilled wind stirs whispers
from the yellow-headed trees.
A little bit of pipe smoke
seasons the afternoon,
which is very still and quiet.
The sun hasn't peeked out
through the blanket of grey sky—
just the blush of its dim light,
all crystalline in the fragility
of a brand new autumn.

Now that it's here,
autumn will burn brightly by
with such color and poignancy.
And so I sit out here in the chill
to watch it all come again—
all the hot colors and cold rot,
all the old crispness
that has seduced poets
since the birth of words.

PAHA KARITUKATEYAPI

The mountain used to talk to me
with countless sylvan voices.
There were ancient songs as I hiked—
primal songs.
Now there are only two songs.

Woodpeckers pound a rhythm.

Thump
  Thump
    Thump

My walking stick pounds a rhythm.

Thump
  Thump
    Thump

It's been seven busy years
since I've trod this familiar trail.
The woods on this mountain
are charred beyond recognition
from the wildfire that ate the slopes
this last summer.
There once were moss and weeds—
wildflowers blooming like gems
in the tall grass.
Now the rust of dead pine needles
blankets the quiet open spaces

that once were green.
As I hike, I touch the burnt trunks
of each pine tree within reach.
I see how death has changed them—
my fingertips are blackened.

This old peak and I,
separated these many years,
have once again communed,
but neither one of us
is the entity we used to be.
We're both so changed now.

I weep on the summit.
I don't cry for the mountain—
not necessarily.
I cry because I've returned to it,
and it has taken me this long
to come back.

Then I look for autumnal leaves
among the blackened ruin
of the mountaintop.
I'll press them between the pages
of my favorite books.

Two woodpeckers followed me
up to the stony summit.

Thump

    Thump

        Thump

PROVIDING

The night has fallen
like an indigo curtain.
The stars above this cold creek
are almost overwhelming to gaze into.
We can see our breath
around the crackling campfire—
bellies warm and full with soup
that we cooked on the coals
and a shared brown trout
that we ate right out of the skillet.
The meat fell right off her bones.
She was aggressive
when she took my lure—
flipping her wet sinuous length
out of the babbling current.
I killed her quickly with my knife
so that she didn't suffer much.
Her guts were lined with yellow roe.
She was a provider, that girl,
and she provides still.

A 2013 RED

I raise a glass to my hawkish nose—
dignified and too large some days.

This dry wine, deeply crimson,
smells of black currant
and of tobacco, oak, and vanilla.

This bottle may not survive
to see the rosy fingers of dawn
sliding through the empty trees.

HANDFULS

This golden morning—
sunrise burning through the fog
and the empty boughs of the trees.
There are several deer in the field,
grazing in the cold dawn—
silhouettes in the yellow murk.
Poetry is rising here in this swell—
this tide of fog and light.
I'm thankful for the deer
and all the weight they carry—
these handfuls of prose
I hold like berries in my hands.

Eat of them and all of this.

Break the bread of this yellow morn,
and dine, my friends,
like hungry wild beasts.

NEW SAVIORS

Was there ever any true goodness
in this flesh of ours at all?
Did it ever shine—
a soft green glow
amongst the sturdy gnarl of our roots?
Could we touch it again
in the rosy womb of a new life?
Oh, I have romance and my work—
I have my memories.
I have my travels and adventures,
and I have the sky and trees—
also a quiet creek.
But I can't help but to feel
that we lost something—
somewhere.
Robert Frost could find it—
Walt Whitman too.
But they've already become
something else.
Our saviors are gone,
and so we must find new ones.
The first place we must search
is, of course, a solemn forest—
smelling of earth and wildness.
The second is a shoreline
under autumnal skies—
a lone lighthouse casting its gleam out
into something dark and stormy—
something only poets can touch.

HIKING HYMNS

There's a burden of snow
and cold wintery shadows
in this forested gorge,
but the gulch still murmurs—
its cool flow not yet locked in ice.
The oak and birch trees here
have shed their gowns
but for the few dry leaves
the color of old leather
that still rattle in the branches.

My ten-year-old child and I
cover nine miles of trail,
and we ascend from a morning
cloaked in the blue gloom of snow
into a bright afternoon
awash in November light
and the airy whispers of the pines.
We're in high country now.

There are hymns out here
in these woods and mountains,
but they're different
from the hymns that you know.
I teach my daughter these hymns—
how to hear the voices.

I teach her to listen.

RAKING THE LEAVES

I'm late in raking the leaves—
it's a Sunday in late November,
within a week of Thanksgiving.
The sky is a heavy grey—
piercingly cold.
It's already snowed once, melted,
and will snow again before December.

The leaves are fossil-colored
and as brittle as cold glass.
They're caught in my scarf
and the grey wool of my pea coat—
I'll pluck them off when I'm done.

I'm raking the piles I began weeks ago.
My kids were helping me then.
It was a sunny day in October.
Afterwards, I drank some champagne
as I read Mary Oliver poems.
I'd stayed outside long enough
for the bright sapphire sky
to burn into rich golden yellow—
a reflection of the leaves
held up in the autumnal trees.

I'm still raking,
but soon I've got the leaves all heaped—
whatever leaves that the crisp wind
hasn't taken with it.
I fill a pair of huge leaf bags,
scooping up armfuls of crunchy leaves
with my bare hands—

the fragrance of earthy decay
and the feel of detritus in my fingers.
My hands are writer's hands—
soft with only a couple callouses.
But my mind is thick with scars.

As I work, I think of writing.
I think about friends I don't see anymore,
and I wonder who burned the bridges—
was it them or I?
I think of Virginia Woolf
and *To the Lighthouse*.
She had plenty of friends,
but she ended up going mad.
Mrs. Woolf is the last thing I think of
before I'm finished bagging the leaves.

I smash the leaf bags down
into our big garbage bin.
I'm breathing heavily when it's done—
sweating even though it's freezing.
I go back to the front of the house—
back to where I raked the leaves.
I can see the lawn now.
It looks dry and dead—
the flaxen color of wheat.
Where the leaves were heaped,
the grass is spring green.

I take a seat in one of the weathered chairs
that we keep by our front step.
The chair groans as I sit in it—
one of these days I'll fall through.
I like to sit out here to read

while I smoke a cigar or a tobacco pipe,
a cold beer or a cocktail in hand.

I pick up my red thermos
full of hot black coffee,
and I take a long drink of it
like it's water—
as though it could relieve my thirst.
Then I light up a flavored cigar
and open a thick book
of Ernest Hemingway short stories.

After a little while,
I take another look at the yard—
smoke slipping from between my lips
in a bluish-grey ribbon.
There are still a few leaves left,
caught in the dry grass
and shivering in the breeze,
but most of the leaves are gone.
Sitting in that old chair,
I avoid most of the wind's cold bite,
and some warmed afternoon sunlight
has settled on my hands.
A pleasant feeling comes over me—
a full contented feeling.

Sundays are about tranquility—
even when it's snowing or raining
or a chilled blanket of cloud
has settled across the sky.
I'm glad that on this Sunday
I raked the leaves,
and that I'm sitting outside afterwards,

finishing a cigar with a Hemingway story
fresh in my head.

I smell the dead leaves everywhere—
especially on my hands.
It's blended with the aroma of coffee
and cigar smoke,
and I'm sure you can smell it now
when you think of it—
the scent of fall.

I wrote some poetry in the morning,
when the rich loud light was spilling
into the living room
through the tall windows.
But after raking those leaves
and reading some Hemingway,
I think I might write a little bit more.

Tonight, after my daughters are asleep
and my wife is reading a novel in bed,
I'll pour some bourbon over ice,
and I'll sit at my desk—
behind my old typewriter.

I'll write a poem.

It might be a very simple poem—
maybe just about raking the leaves
on a Sunday afternoon
in late November.

THE NEW HOUSE

This first sunrise—
a young firmament
of citrusy rose tones.

The blue spruces
are pale with frost.

Our old bookshelves
stand in the living room.
Hemingway, Carver, Tolstoy—
all my old friends.

Already, I am at home.

NEW YEARS EVE IN DENVER

We're driving south from the High Plains.
There are the city lights of Denver—
the winter sun low behind the Rockies
that are wreathed in snow.
The rugged horizon smolders orange
and is smeared up into lavender.
Up there in those cool tones
is a fine crescent moon—
the last of the year.
A flock of geese passes in front of it,
but we're driving, and I can't hear them.

Later, we're breaking bread
at the home of our dear friends—
Crawfish Étouffée over dirty rice.
We all have gin cocktails—
local stuff infused with lavender.
Talking politics with likeminded people—
a table of open minds and open hearts.
In the diverse landscape of the city
we don't have to hide who we are
like we do back home.
Then we descend to the basement
for a private musical performance—
more of a meditative ritual than song.
The lights are turned low.
Everyone's holding someone else—
there's love here in the warmth.

I feel high—
entranced.

There are lemony evergreen notes
of smoldering Palo Santo wood
in the thick mystical dark.
We burn away the things
to be left behind with 2016—
I watch *hopelessness* go up
in sudden orange flames.

In the quiet morning
at another friend's house
I can still smell the scent
of that holy Palo Santo wood
on my fingertips.
It wasn't all a dream.

This dawn is timeless—
ancient.

But it is also something young.

BUKOWSKI ON A THURSDAY NIGHT

I'm reading Charles Bukowski
on a Thursday night—
savoring the spit and vitriol.
I drink a bottle of stout beer
as I eat the chaotic lines.
My right hand turns the pages,
and my fingers smell like cigar smoke
from earlier in the day.

As the lines disappear I wonder
how many years will pass me by
before I read these lines again.

Where will my life be?

How many new poems
will I have written?

Will my wife still love me?

Will I finally love myself?

How many yellowed Octobers
will have bloomed and rotted—
sunset breaking through branches
in a tide of honeyed light—
the hard ground brittle
with all the fallen leaves?

UNPRECEDENTEDLY

It's Friday the 13th,
but I haven't forgotten
how to love unbearably.
We just discovered
that there's a faint pulse of life
in the depths of her womb—

      unprecedentedly.

We'd given up any hope
that a child could possibly happen
between the two of us.
We'd prepared our lives
for it not to happen.
The doctors said it wouldn't—
ovaries swollen with cysts
said that it wouldn't.

But then, all at once,
after seven years together,
everything is changing.

      Everything is changing.

      Everything.

A QUIET DAY IN JANUARY

It's a Sunday afternoon,
and I'm leaning against a railing
on the back deck.
There are trails forged by my dogs
crisscrossing the snow in the yard—
their eternal hunt for fleeing rabbits
is scrawled in the white.
Leaning forward against the railing,
I thumb through the newest issue
of *The Saturday Evening Post*,
and I smoke a dry knot of flake
from one of my tobacco pipes.
I make January smell like autumn.
Eventually I amble back inside,
take off my wet hiking boots,
and sit down to a plate of eggs
whipped up by my wife.
I make sure each jiggly bite
is dashed in pepper and sea salt.
Warm white sunlight
slants through the big windows.
The dogs slumber like drunks
in the bright pools of radiance—
even they don't want today to end.

ANN

for my mother

My third daughter
will be born in September.
Her middle name will be Ann—
the same middle name as my mother's,
who, like me,
was also the youngest of three.

My mother, even when she was young
and raising three children
with a fun and irresponsible husband,
clutched at the frayed edges of our household—
wrapped it around us kids
like a warm blanket.
Secure.
We didn't know how she struggled
to give us what we needed,
how she endeavored to enrich us
with books and history
and experiences that are written in me still.

My third daughter
will be born in September.

And her middle name will be Ann.

A DAY OFF

In the basement
reading Beat poetry
by firelight—
Wordsworth tomorrow.

Shaking words down
like wild apples
from the branch.

HONEY ON A LEAF

I've been looking all winter,
but with no luck.
There's honey somewhere
dripping from a leaf
that hasn't rotted away.
People are feeding from it,
and their souls are swelling
with sweet amber earthiness.
They find it easily, but I cannot.
I'm eating snow and ice—
a bottle of cold beer to wash it down.
I'm not out there blooming
with vigor and wildness,
like everyone else.
I'm disintegrating—
stagnation, domesticity,
starving for nature,
starving for travel.

I will suffer greatly
before this is over.

I won't be the same.

THE ABANDONED HOUSE

It's a freezing night.
I walk inside carefully and slowly
as though I could disturb someone—
perhaps a forlorn ghost.

Windows long devoid of panes—
paint chipping from the frames.

A woman's single shoe.

Snow drifts on vintage carpet—
a razor-sharp winter wind
slicing through the rooms.

The light from my flashlight
glitters across the rime
in a vacant bedroom
that had long ago forgotten
the beautiful urgency of loving.

YOUR WATER

We are cracked open—
        exposed.

Beautifully exposed.

Rivers pour forth.
Your water meets my water.

CLARITY

The last of the dark blue glow
is falling from the overcast sky.
The pines place ragged silhouettes
against the cold canvas of the night.
It's been pissing a fine rain
throughout most of the empty day,
and I'm reading Dostoevsky
by the yellowed light of a lamp.
I'm aware of what's happening to me—
simplicity and honesty settling
like a hooded cloak of heavy wool,
keeping me warm and dry.
My life is a changing thing—
a brand-new thing.
I've been rattled to my roots,
and I'll never be the same.
I've been scrubbed clean,
and I'm seeing everything
in a fresh clarifying light.
I am the Prince, the "Idiot"
wandering about in fresh purity—
unable to be anything but genuine.
There she is, my beloved wife.
She's sitting across the room—
as lovely as ever—
our child growing within her.
This winter tested us,
but our love for one another
is growing around us, solidifying,

encasing us in ageless crystal
that nothing and nobody can sunder.
I'm unmoored from the man that I was—
from the things I thought were needed
to achieve contentment and happiness.

There she is.

She is that perfect autumnal hike.
She is the prose from my pen.
She is the paint on my fingers.
She is a friend's kind word.

She is that beautiful old city
that I have never seen.

SUNRISE IN LITTLE HAVANA

Miami—
early morning.

A pastel sunrise through the window
at a breakfast joint.

Palm fronds gently waving—
leaves shivering.

A citrus breeze.

Everyone is speaking Spanish.

Our waitress is Cuban—
her curves would give it away
if her accent didn't.

I dip my toast into yolk.

MONROE COUNTY PILGRIMAGE

These islands—
strung southwest
into the Gulf of Mexico
like a string of green pearls.
We're driving to the end
of U.S. Route 1.

My wife is sleeping
in the seat next to me,
and my daughters slumber
in the backseat—
mouths agape like little drunks.
They're missing this,
but that's all right.
They'll see it again in a few days
when we drive back to Miami.

Out in the middle
of Seven Mile Bridge,
you can't see land
in either direction.
It's just the turquoise sea—
our red rental car gliding
down that elevated ribbon
of roadway.

Little Duck Key—
we're in the Lower Keys now.

Family still slumbering—
I pull the car into a gas station
so I can take a leak.
There're puddles of rainwater
in the parking lot
from a morning shower.
Thick green palm fronds
are pressing in from all sides.

A rooster struts around.

He's an old hand
at living a quiet life
down in the Keys.

And I'm just a student here—
a pilgrim making his way.

THESE MOMENTS

They went to the Florida Keys
so he could hold her in the sea—
her legs wrapped around him
and his hands on her ass.
They kiss hard and deep—
waves push and pull them.
Gulls wheel overhead—
a pelican perches on a pier.
In the privacy of the warm water
their hands explore each other.

They have these moments.

They make time for them—
seek them out—
set aside money for them.

These moments are worth it.

KEY WEST MORNING

After the storm, the sea was green,
but now, the next morning,
the sea is aquamarine
and the hot sun drifts
in a bath of pure blue—
paradise colors.

The island is speaking to me
through the hotel room window—
voices of wind, sea, and sand.

I still smell of yesterday's sunscreen,
and my short hair is unruly
from the salt of the ocean water—
I don't feel like washing it off me.

People are crisscrossing the streets
on pastel-colored cruiser bikes—
making their way to beaches,
to places to eat breakfast,
or to tourist spots—
maybe to the Southernmost Point
or perhaps up to Islamorada
to fish like Hemingway.

The iguanas are stirring
in the warm morning light—
clinging to branches
with long claws.

Roosters are crowing
and strutting all over the island—
looking down, I see a hen,
a line of chicks following her.

The leather poetry journal
that I bought on Martha's Vineyard
rests upon the room's glossy desk
beside a few brightly-colored pens—
colors for Key West poems—
aqua, bright green, and neon pink.
Sunglasses also rest upon the desk—
grains of sand still stuck to them.

I brought some Gogol to read,
but reading Russian literature
seems absurd in the trade winds.
The Old Man and the Sea
would've been more sensible.

The tides were up early this morning—
probably earlier than anything else.
The waves never sleep—
never cease feeling the shore.

Anybody a little bit broken
could be healed by Key West.

I'm being made whole
just by waking up here
and staring out the window.

THE HOUSE ON WHITEHEAD STREET

dedicated to Ernest Hemingway

"I want to get to Key West and away from it all."
—Ernest Hemingway, *Selected Letters*

Walking through the still rooms
of your old house on Whitehead Street.
Passing through the life of a dead man—
not a faraway deity.
You're so real it's terrifying—
I'm still trying to make sense of it.

That old rod and reel—
you used them out on *Pilar*.
Those typewriters,
especially that one in your office—
your prose sprouted from them
like blooms of ink and honesty.
You read all those hardcover books—
wrote in some of them.
That little tub in the bathroom—
you washed in it.

You laughed here, cried maybe—
once or twice.
You loved and hated here.
You fought with Pauline here—
made love to her in that bed
that's now chained off.

Some six-toed cats sleep in it now
as they surely did then—
when this island was a quieter place.

PURIFICATION

Pines—
high mountain air.

Quiet trails.
The gloom of the wood.

Emptiness.

My old soul wanders
down to the sand and sea—
the near turquoise
and that dark heavy blue
farther out.

Soiled hands
gather seawater.

I wash the moss
from my pale skin
with the salt of the sea.

I bury my heart
on the breezy shore
before I return
to the high country.

A WOLF I MET

Rain had been falling all day.

A timber wolf ambled past the car,
within touching distance—
his brown coat was sodden.
His wide paws flattened
against the black asphalt of the road
with each heavy step.

I watched him silently pass by,
and he bent the rich amber
of his wise primal eyes
into my own—
eyes that were humbled and less wise.

I know, I felt like saying to him.

I absolutely know.

LINES WRITTEN IN EARLY MAY

I raise a cigar to my thin lips—
my belly full of warm dinner.
I'm watching the sunshine turn
in a halo of smoke—
it dims to a luminescent amber
as it falls between some tall pines
in the neighbor's yard.
In our yard, one of my daughters
is climbing a young aspen tree.
She marvels at all the bright green leaves
that have seemingly bloomed overnight.

Spring happens fast, I tell her.

And it makes everything look so pretty, she adds.

Wyoming has a richness to it, sure,
but I'd give it up in an instant
for Martha's Vineyard or Key West—
one of those quaint precious islands
upon which I scattered pieces of my soul.
I scatter myself on faraway shores
like my grandpa's ashes were scattered
at the sixth hole of the local golf course.

A man's soul knows its home.

FROM A HAMMOCK AT SAND CREEK

I put up a hammock
between a pair of oak trees,
and now I'm sipping a can of beer
and writing some lines in my journal.

The creek's close by—
my wife and kids scaring the trout
on a scorching spring day.
The fly fishing is shit anyway—
in this bitch of a sun.
My fly rod leans against a tree.
I know I'm sunburned already,
but that's all right.

That's camping.

God, how these wilds
were a sort of siren to me!
I craved them like an addict.
I still appreciate them—
truly I do.
But I just don't need them
in the way that I used to.
Winter is always a harsh teacher,
and it has educated me.

I need other things.

I need those daughters
that are screeching happily
as they brave the cold creek.
I need that gorgeous woman
wading out there with them—
my third daughter growing
in that sacred womb.

A ladybug lands on me.
The hammock gently sways,
and I know now
how to be this person
that I've always needed to be.

I'm more solid than stone.

I am the convergence
of all the paths of man.

GREY GHOST

for Laynee

My sister said I should write of you—
our old horse, pale grey,
strolling the green paddock
between our house and the pond
in rural Rappahannock County.
She remembers you better than I—
you're more childhood scenery to me
than anything substantial.
I rode you only a few times,
and never without her watching—
making sure I was safe
and that I was riding you properly.
But you were important to her,
the second girl I ever loved,
and thus a fitting subject for honest lines.

TRUTH

When I was thirteen
I stole a book.
Big things have tiny beginnings.
Lifelong journeys start with single steps—
a theft was mine.
It was an old black hardcover
comprised of dense colorless prose—
an encyclopedic and academic book
of the ancient teachings of Buddha.
I was in a religious hangover at the time—
fresh from fearfully reading the *Book of Revelation*
and from a ritualistic stint as an altar boy
in a small town Catholic church.
I was weary of being intimidated
by antiquated doctrine
designed to terrify ancient civilizations.
I was weary of long-dead people
claiming to be prophets.
I was needy—
seeking.

And now, all these years later,
I'm still seeking—
still running my fingers
through the shallow ineffectual sands
of so many different paths.
I think I want enlightenment,
but I'm not sure anymore
what exactly that even means,

or if it's even attainable.
I know that I'll desire and suffer.
I know I want to feel—
always.
In these last twenty years
of my aimless wanderings for truth
I'm not sure if I've discovered
one single thing about truth,
except that I don't believe gods exist.
But maybe demigods exist—
however, they're all writers,
and most of them are dead.

But Buddhism though—
I keep finding myself
touching my initial footprints
away from Judeo-Christian doctrine
and trying to see that eastern glow
that so many others have found.
I wear a mala—
black onyx beads these days.
I say some mantras sometimes—
not because I feel anything special
from rolling those foreign holy words
around in my mouth,
but because I hope that someday
I might.
I used to burn incense
and chant in shadowy comfort—
can still recall the sweet earthy scents
of "Tibetan Lotus" and "One Love."
I used to meditate,

but I haven't in several years—
it's something that I misplaced
and can't quite locate again.

One night, when I was nineteen
and living in a terribly small apartment,
I couldn't sleep at all
before the first day of a new job.
And so, after tears of frustration
and wanting to pull out my fucking hair,
I started meditating.
I meditated the entire night—
deep meditation.
I found myself standing in a place
of high winds and tall yellow-brown grass—
perfect rotund hills.
The sky was like bright burnished gold—
a summer sunset with no sun.
There were giant beings made of stone—
they were lumbering around the brassy hills,
and their unintelligible words were deep.
The words could just barely be separated
from the sounds of the wind.
I walked those yellowish hills
with those wandering stone colossi—
I didn't feel any need to fear them.
In a silk robe that fluttered in the winds,
I stood in the tall undulating grass.

In all the years since,
I haven't been able to find my way back
to that mysterious place,

and it feels like I've stopped trying.
Maybe I doubt now that it was real—
perhaps I fell asleep in the lotus position
and dreamed it all up in a mystic stupor
in some early morning hour.

And that old book on Buddhism,
the one that started me
on this intensely lonely sojourn—
I threw it in a dumpster
on an airbase in Qatar
the day before I nearly died—
face numb and swollen and blue.
The truth is like air,
and I'm still trying to draw breath.

My wife, she asks me sometimes
why it's still necessary for me to keep looking
for some spiritual truth that's barely discernible
and that slips through my clutching fingers
like ribbons of campfire smoke.
I don't know how to answer her.
I just don't have any idea
why I'm still seeking for something—
still wandering these paths
that branch out from the misty roots
of the first story ever told.
It was a story told by a feral man
without a written or spoken language
in some prehistoric epoch.
On the wall of some cave,
he told a story of magic and stars—

of a great hunt.

Maybe, I'm just trying to find my way back
to that very first story—
the only real truth there ever was.

LATE NIGHT SNACK

Husband and wife
falling asleep—
both with books of poems
instead of smartphones.

Half asleep—
lines of poetry
blooming within me
like candlelight.

Fully asleep—
sometimes,
but only briefly.

Outside, the dog barks—
shrill explosion.

Don't leave me, she pleads.

I'll be back.

Always come back to me, she says,
half-awake and fading fast.

Okay.

He smiles—
kisses her forehead.

Cornbread muffins—
cooled off now,
resting on the counter.
A can of ginger ale—
too late for beer.

Rain is pouring.

Hush, quiet house—
still house—
slumbering house
at midnight.

In the dark hallway—
a naked doll.
On the antique desk—
a beautiful old typewriter,
and a glowing desk lamp.
Turn it off.

Clean up.
Take a piss.

Back to the bed.

Back to her.

AGING

Afternoon rain—
camping by a waterfall.
The calm crash of the falling creek—
that steady choir of gravity.
Sunshine then—
a June breeze.
The waterfall glitters molten
in that hot western sunshine—
hottest part of the day still to come.

A red-handled saw in the tall grass,
still wet from the rain—
the blade's rusted in some spots,
but its teeth still work just fine.

I wade out in the creek
and pull stones up out of the mud—
pile them on the shore.
Wife changing clothes in the tent—
the French cast of her bare flesh.

Crackling campfire—
coils of aromatic smoke.
In the light of my headlamp,
tilted down so I can read
in the wild June night,
I can see my breath.

Silvery liquid moon—

the current glitters like diamonds.
A lone white-faced cow
stands atop a moonlit hill.
Waterfall music—
slumber.

Morning quietude—
dawn floods through green leaves.
A newly-lit fire.
I eat a juicy peach—
beard sticky with sugars.
Brown sugar bacon in the skillet—
cooked on the hot embers.
We hold one another for a little while
on the quiet trail beside the creek.
And then a midmorning fuck in the tent—
desires finally quenched.

Hammock now, overlooking the water—
reading poems in the warming light.
A long stem of green grass
is clenched in my teeth.
The waterfall still roars—
the deep creek flows from it
like a crystalline wound,
touches of green and brown.
The aging morning—
an unseen bird sings.
Pale and indefinite—
the day's first cloud drifts
over the pines on the southern ridge.
In the high grass on the far bank

a silent heron, impossibly huge,
takes flight and passes over the trees.

A short nap in the hammock—
awaken to my wife swimming.
The majesty of existence.
This life is shimmering—
unbelievably full.

Today I am certainly older,
and I am thankful for it.

DOGS

dedicated to Rigby

In the morning
we had three dogs,
but in the evening
only one dog was left.

Earlier, I'd washed the blood
from the face and paws
of the aggressor.
She was wildly submissive
as I wiped her fur,
and she seemed almost happy—
her one brown eye and her one blue—
as we drove to the Animal Control Center—
green grasslands spilling by
and in the bluish distance—
Devils Tower erect like a thumb.

But earlier than all that,
I dug a grave in the corner of our yard
for the diminutive victim—
the rictus of her frozen maw
filling with black flies.
I wept helplessly as I put her in a towel
and placed her body in the earth.
She had been scared all her life,
but on the other side
of a painful and brutally violent moment
she wouldn't need to be scared again.

It wasn't until much later—
one confused and lonely dog
left to wander the rooms and yard,
looking for his friends in a fog of loss—
that I finally washed the stink of blood
and the sourness of death
from my shaking hands.

I awoke in the middle of the night
to the incredibly mournful howls
of our one remaining dog.
I went outside with him,
under the pale light of the moon,
so that he could scour the backyard
for wherever it was
that his two friends were hiding.

FADING

The dark pines in the rain—
scent of dusk.

The rain stops just long enough
to see a scarlet ribbon of light
blush beyond the trees—
a swell of fire and blood.

Downpour—
the light fades entirely.

Thunder crashes.

Lightning flickers to the south—
over the darkened prairie.

Far beyond the storm,
the moon, just now,
is fading from full—
strawberry moon
becomes something else.

GREEN THUMB

A garden has grown wild
on the edge of the yard.

Untamed.

Little red raspberries.
Birds have eaten the corn
off the dry crunchy stalks.

The ground is a spongy loam
of nutritious compost—
thick and fragrant
with last year's forgotten harvest.
I can still see the tomatoes—
yellow-orange skins
fading into the ground
as if through osmosis.
Small gelatinous pumpkins
squat in the greenery like severed heads—
pale and slowly imploding.

The natural wildness of it all
excites me.

I would feel guilt
to exert my own order upon it,
but my father-in-law had a green thumb
before drunkenness rotted it off.
Maybe my wife inherited it.

She could use this garden.

POSTCOITAL

Night has fallen.

She slumbers in the other room.

I'm stirring whole milk
into a mug of Irish breakfast tea
with a small teaspoon
that I ordered from England
several years ago—
back when I was reading Thomas Hardy.

A train passes through town
as I take another sip.

SMILING WIND

Inside—
cool shadows.
A silent summer kitchen
in complete stillness.
The backdoor's open—
a morning breeze sneaks in
and giggles down the hall.

God, how I miss them—
the top two chambers of my heart.

God, how I take that name in vain
as the trashcan swallows
another empty can of beer.

This is my Saturday—
this is my sunny afternoon
that's too old already.
She and I sleep it away
like cats in the lukewarm shade
of a house closed off
from the rest of the world.

Smiling wind isn't smiling anymore—
the backdoor's closed,
and that morning was used up
hours and hours ago.

ELEVEN MILE CANYON

Thick banks of grey fog
sweep into the canyon
like knives—
cutting slopes of pine
to darkened ribbons.
The sun is swallowed
by the cold grim night
up in the mountains.
Clouds scrape low
over the canyon—
bleeding a fine rain.

OVERLOOK TRAIL

for Dylan Rupe

Granite outcropping
at the top of the trail—
overlooking the valley.

Wild strawberries and raspberries
growing up out of the cracks
in the granite—
some other fragrant herb
we don't recognize.

Bright green lichens
and the glister of quartz
upon the stone.

SIREN OF THE ROCKIES

She makes her way
across the cold stream
as she eats an apple—
belly swollen with child.

Three crows battle overhead—
rainbow trout conquer the current.

She reaches a dry boulder
at the far side of the water,
and takes a seat as she finishes
her piece of sweet fruit.

FELLOWSHIP

for Paul, Chase, Patrick, and Dylan

There is song rising up
into the thin mountain air
at nine thousand feet—
rising also through the pines
that filter the white eye
of warm summer light.
One of my brothers
glistens the sky with his soul
as he strums his acoustic guitar—
he calls in a cool breeze.
I watch with my other brothers—
poets, musicians, and adventurers.
We have been pulled from far places
to come finally together
in the wild loft of America.
There are stars shining
upon the denim of my jeans
and the skin of my hands—
it's from the quartz in the dirt
that we're all sharing
for just this one brief moment.

HEADED HOME

Yellow sun settles
behind the high mountains
off in the western haze.
Lavender clouds—
some pink in the air beneath them.
We're driving north
on a Sunday evening,
and I am so fulfilled.

At twilight—
only an orange glow left—
there are some vibrant fireworks
over a small Wyoming town.
The fine hook of the crescent moon
becomes a pearly orange hue
as it slips into the horizon—
hot on the heels
of the fallen dusk.

LIKE STORMS

In bed,
they gazed at one another.

Your eyes are really grey today.

Not blue? he inquired,
motioning to his blue shirt—
his eyes typically swayed
from green to blue
and from blue to green
based on the color
of his clothes.

No, they're like storms.

The storms came later—
with rain and hail
and a frenzied wind
that jostled the trees.

She was gone then,
and he was alone
with the dog and cat.

A bolt of blue lightning
sang in the north.

The storms broke apart
after a little while
and fell away to the east—
the sinking sun shone golden
through the wet leaves

of the honey locust.

He walked barefoot
through the sodden grass
that was soft and plush
beneath his pale steps.

He touched the sunlight
that was stretched like honey
through the glistening boughs.

After the storms were done,
bats were swooping
low over the yard—
chewing mosquitos
right out of the damp air.
The cat watched, hungry.

The rounded mammatus clouds
were tinged peach
in the dwindling dusk.

She would be home soon—
the storms were over.

And his eyes—
maybe they were a new color.

CORNFLOWERS OF AKULINA

dedicated to Ivan Turgenev

He awakens beneath a birch tree
in the kind hours before evening,
and the September woods
are flooded with light.
He had fallen asleep
taking shelter from a light rain.
There's a girl close by,
but she doesn't notice him.
She is lovely and young,
and she waits for someone—
tears are drying
on the soft tan of her cheek.
A secret sadness
trembles within her—
expectant—
daring to hope.

In her gentle hand—
marigolds and wild costmary
and a little bundle of cornflowers—
bright blue and bound
with slender grass.

IN THESE QUIET HOURS

for Story

It was a cold cloudy Saturday
in the heart of September
when you met us—
not sobbing,
but just looking around
with your large active eyes.
You are a calm and kind soul—
you didn't even cry
when you were washed up
by young diligent nurses.
Everything changed for you,
and the beautiful fierceness of light
and sharpened sounds
became this whole new reality—
a bit cold perhaps,
but absolutely pulsing
with wonder and adoration.

And now, later,
Mother is slumbering in bed,
attached to her machines—
blue screens spilling their light
into the darkened hospital room.
You are bundled up
in my protective arms—
sleeping heavily like your mother
and cooing so very softly.
I hold you in these quiet hours
in the darkness of early morning,
and very silently and peacefully
you settle into the one chamber

remaining in my heart.

And I am made entirely whole.

PURE LAND (WHERE I'LL BE)

I'm not lost.

I'm going to be all right,
and I'll be waiting for you.

There'll be the squeak of splitting pine
as I chop up a little firewood
outside of a good sturdy cabin
that was waiting for me here—
in this old-growth forest
of oaks and evergreens.
The nights here are quite cool,
but the days are sunny and warm
except when I wish for rain.
At dawn, there is always a fog
that swells with the sunrise.
Nearby there's a quiet stream—
it has no name,
but it's thick with trout.
Nothing here really has a name
except for myself,
and you'll have your name too
whenever it is that you arrive.

I don't have a television here,
just shelves full of literature—
all my favorites.
But whenever you show up,
I'm sure we can dig up a television—
maybe somewhere in the cellar.
The fridge is always loaded with food—
meats, cheeses, fruits, and vegetables

that never seem to spoil
and are always replenished.
There's always an aroma in my cabin
of something being baked,
and there's always a good pie
or fresh loaves of homemade bread
cooling on the counter—
a clean bread knife beside them.
The decanters are never shallow
of good bourbon and gin.

I'll have a fire going in the hearth,
keeping the cabin nice and cozy,
and I'll be sitting in a chair
out on the front porch—
reading some Hemingway
or perhaps some Jim Harrison
or Raymond Carver.
Those dead writers
don't feel so far away anymore—
not like they used to.
In that chair on the porch,
I'll cover my legs
with a flannel blanket,
and I'll be smoking a pipe
filled with good fresh tobacco.
And, of course, I'll have a full belly—
the smoke won't make me nauseated.

When I finally wrap my arms around you,
my beard will smell of pipe smoke,
and my eyes will be bright.

This is where I'll be

as I wait patiently to see you
walking towards me through the trees
and the effulgent morning fog.

But don't you be in a hurry—
you just take your time,
and don't you dare worry for me.

I'm going to be just fine,
and this is where I'll be.

THINK OF ME

A dusk stroll through Edgartown—
crisp autumn air dim and sparkling.
The charming streetlights shone
along the brick sidewalk.

Between the big white houses
we could see the harbor
in the fading blush of the day—
the lighthouse we walked to
only a short while before.

The next day we explored Main Street
before going to the pub for lunch.
I bought you two pairs
of antique earrings—
one orange like October leaves,
and one seafoam green like the tide.

Think of me, will you,
when they dance along your jawline.

ENCORE

I'm not sure how to write
of all the different things I've let go—
of all the changes that have occurred.
But I suppose I'm not entirely sure
if it's necessary to write of them.
You can see me outside,
reading in the afternoon sun—
writing now, I guess.
I'm sure you can feel
how I've become a well of gravity—
immobile, resolute, committed.
And I hold all the precious things
around me like a colorful bouquet.

I'm breathing it all in—
I'm breathing this life in.

I am not afraid.

My god—
I am not afraid.

I wish to acknowledge the following publications where these poems first appeared:

River Ram Press, 2016: "A Little History"

Selcouth Station, 2017: "Full," "Postcoital," "Trying to Get to Abu Nakhlah"

Poetryhub, 2017: "This Isn't a Poem"

Doorway to Art, Nov.-Dec. issue, 2017: "Tombstones at Edgartown," "Cusp," "Nature Words," "Soup in the Desert," "Sparks," "Nighttime in Qatar," "Of Moss and Soil," "Key West Morning," "Late Night Snack," "Sunrise in Little Havana"

ACKNOWLEDGMENTS

I want to thank my friends and family, my publisher and editor, and the writers and poets that continue to inspire me: Ernest Hemingway, Jim Harrison, Mary Oliver, Raymond Carver, Gary Snyder, Ted Kooser, Robert Frost, Henry David Thoreau, Ivan Turgenev, and Leo Tolstoy.

ABOUT THE AUTHOR

Nicholas Trandahl is an avid outdoorsman and credits his many adventures and travels as the prime source of inspiration for his writings. One is just as likely to find him on a trail or beside a trout stream as sitting at his writing desk with his old typewriter, a family heirloom. Trandahl lives in Wyoming with his wife and children.

Made in the USA
Coppell, TX
06 April 2022

76144837R00088